Parables DECODED Of Jesus

Study Guide

*Unveiling the Mysteries of God's Kingdom
through the Stories of Jesus*

Volume 2: Old and New

Hany & Diana Asaad

Relentless Publications

ISBN:978-0-9983999-2-8
ISBN10:0-9983999-2-2

DEDICATION

To Lily, Grace, and Hannah, you encourage us at every step to pursue Jesus relentlessly.

To our fellow sojourners.
May the stories Jesus told guide us all deeper into His fullness.

To all of our Parables Decoded participants and encouragers, thank you for praying for us and making these books a reality!

CONTENTS

WELCOME

Welcome to *Parables Decoded*!

Parables Decoded is a six-week journey in understanding the stories Jesus told in the context of His lifetime and applying His lessons to our lives.

Each session explores a different aspect of a parable through the lens of culture by digging deeper into the stories Jesus told. Lessons are composed of Bible study, and video and small group discussions that pulls out the richer applications. However, the real decoding happens after the video when you dive into each topic during guided small group time. Through the group discussion and the short homework, true transformation begins to unfold.

How To Use This Guide

As you'll discover, the parables of Jesus are practical. This study is designed to provide the tools so you can develop a closer spiritual walk with Jesus.

These truths will help you understand the often misinterpreted principles that have significant transforming power. Each session begins with a Bible passage, followed by explanation of the parable, and cultural relevance. The next section uncovers the reason for this parable, followed by the parable's composition, and then discussion. We wrap up each weekly study with the conclusion and homework. *Parables Decoded* moves fast, and the homework is not mandatory but highly encouraged.

The real growth in this study will happen during your small group time. There, you will process the content of the message, ask questions, and learn from others as you share what God is doing in your lives through the parables. Each session contains a bonus Middle-Eastern recipe for you to experiment and experience together if you'd like and allow the flavors of the era to cross cultures and connect us to the passages and one another.

This fill-in-the-blank guide lets you follow along together as a group while watching the videos. Answers are provided in the back.

Parables **dΞC0ƆΞD** of Jesus

Introduction to the Parables of Jesus

"But without a parable He did not speak to them." (Mark 4:34)

Stories. They define our lives. They connect us in ways that nothing else can. History and facts seem alive and relevant when sprinkled with stories. Perhaps that is why our Lord used stories to connect deep spiritual truths to everyday occurrences.

God speaks to us in many different forms in the Bible. Scripture is filled with allegories, poetry, prophecy, apocalyptic literature, and parables.

Jesus was intentional about his use of parables to convey deep spiritual truths in relevant stories that were easy for the people of the day to understand. Studying the parables is tremendously beneficial to us today, as well. Jesus made His deep messages pertinent and easy to remember. We might forget principles, but we remember stories. Parables help us apply

1

Biblical philosophies through easy-to-remember stories because we relate to them.

When Jesus spoke in parables, people understood the message more clearly than if He had spoken in plain truths. By digging into the customs of Jesus' day, we can have the same insights.

Let's begin to see the parables as if God were opening a small window to His Kingdom so we get to peek in. The parables provide the greatest insight to know God's heart.

Though Jesus was born in a small town and worked as a carpenter, when He spoke, it was with authority and He AMAZED everyone. Matthew 7:28-29 tells us, "[28]And so it was, when Jesus had ended these sayings, that the people were astonished at His teaching, [29]for He taught them as one having authority, and not as the scribes (NKJV)".

Jesus used ordinary people as the characters of His parables, so everyone was able to understand and relate to the story. Jesus customized His messages and used familiar things like seeds, soil and sheep to illustrate challenging truths.

For example, Jesus used a son who left his father's house and spent all his inheritance and showed the father who missed him (Luke 15:20). Jesus used a shepherd who takes care of sheep (Luke 15:4), He used a farmer who planted seeds (Matthew 13:3), and a fisherman casting nets (Matthew 13:48). Jesus spoke of a wounded man who was robbed (Luke 10:33), a widow (Luke 18:3), and a builder (Luke 14:28). He used a poor man (Luke 16:19), rich man (Luke 12:13-21), servant (Matthew 18:21-35), master (Matthew 25:14-30), and even a king (Matthew 22:1-4).

Therefore Jesus was able to touch on all aspects of life such as familial issues (Luke 15:20), agricultural life (Luke 13:6-9), investing (Matthew 25:14-30), and even politics (Luke 19:11-27) to name a few.

Parables were used by others to convey messages, but the parables of Jesus don't use imaginary, unrealistic characters like trees talking or animals speaking. Jesus is the way, the truth and life (John 14:6). His parables are good for all mankind in every generation. Jesus said in John 6:63, "The words that I speak to you are spirit, and *they* are life."

Key Elements of the Parables

1. During the ministry of Jesus, He _____ to the people in parables.

2. Jesus spoke _____ parables in the New Testament, depending on how you categorize them. For example, in Luke 5:36, we see the parables of the new and old garments and the old and new wineskins, which can be

considered one parable. But in Luke 15 Jesus uses the term "either" between the stories.

3. The parables of Jesus represent about _____ of His preaching.

4. Parables were the most _____ teachings in people's minds.

5. We can extract at least one _____ lesson from each parable.

6. Each and every parable requires a _____ from us. God might want us to start or stop something.

7. Parables can be categorized in three sections:

    a. Relationship and responsibilities between _____ and you, and also _____ toward God.

    b. Relationship and responsibilities between you and your fellow _____.

    c. The believer's responsibilities toward _____- believers.

4 Questions that Frequently Arise about the Parables:

1. What does "parable" _____ ?
2. What are the _____?
3. Why did Christ _____ in parables?
4. How do we _____ the parables?

Q1. What does "parable" mean?

The word "parable" means:

1. The Greek word "Parabole" (Parra-Bo-lay) means to "_____ beside or _____ alongside."
2. Parable means "_____" or "_____like."
3. Parable can also mean _____.

Definition of Parable: A "parable" is an _____ story by which *a familiar idea is cast beside an unfamiliar idea* in such a way that the _____ helps people to better understand and grasp the unfamiliar idea.

Q2. What are the parables of Jesus?

Parables are:

1. Lessons taken from _____ or situations in _____.
2. Typically_____and_____ with powerful meaning, parables teach difficult truths in a simple way.
3. Based in the context of _____ and _____.

4. _____ stories that have a _____ meaning.

5. A way of concealing _____ for believers to uncover.

6. A comparison of two things or two stories for the purpose of _____.

7. Putting something known beside something unknown to _____ the differences.

8. Relatable to _____ because they are common, ordinary stories.

Matthew13:10-13, *"¹⁰ The disciples came to him and asked, "Why do you speak to the people in parables?"* *¹¹ He replied, "Because the knowledge of the **secrets** of the kingdom of heaven has been given to you, but not to them"* *(NIV, emphasis added).*

Q3. Why did Christ speak in parables?

1. Because of the _____ his followers showed to hear and understand God's words.

   "Such large crowds gathered around Him that He got into a boat and sat in it, while all the people stood on the shore" (Matthew 13:2 NIV).

6

2. Because of the people's _____ hearts and unwillingness to _____.

> *"14In them is fulfilled the prophecy of Isaiah: "'You will be ever hearing but never understanding; you will be ever seeing but never perceiving. 15For this people's heart has become calloused" (Matthew 13:14-15 NIV).*

3. To show us how _____ we are.

> *"For truly I tell you, many prophets and righteous people longed to see what you see but did not see it, and to hear what you hear but did not hear it" (Matthew 13:17 NIV).*

4. To _____ those who want to know the truth from everyone else.

> *"36Then Jesus sent the multitude away and went into the house. And His disciples came to Him, saying, "Explain to us the parable of the tares of the field" (Matthew13:36 NKJV).*

Parables catch us off guard and teach us about our sin in a way that will not make us defensive. The Old Testament prophet, Nathan, used a parable to convict King David of his sin. Nathan told the unsuspecting David what appeared to be a harmless story of a rich man and a poor man living in the same city (2 Samuel 12:14). The poor man owned only a single little ewe lamb he loved as a household pet while the rich man possessed large flocks; yet when the wealthy farmer had a guest to serve, he seized the poor man's single lamb for the dinner! Nathan sought to get around David's guarded exterior and cut the bonds of his self-deception to strike the moral blindness that had been veiling his vision. In a sense, Nathan's illustration was a well-laid trap because David responded with moral outrage, thus condemning himself. Nathan then applied the parable to the King's affair with Bathsheba (2 Samuel 12:5-14).

Q4. How do we interpret the parables?

You have to understand the reason Jesus chose the parable. We can interpret the parable based on the incident that caused Jesus to use the parable.

1. _____ each parable thoroughly and carefully. Look for the main truth being uncovered in the parable.

2. Do not hastily apply the _____ of one parable to another. In the parable of the sower, the seed represents the Word of God and the soil represents the human heart (Matthew 13:3-8, 18-23). However, in the

very next parable – the parable of the tares – the seed represents the children of the Kingdom and the field represents the world (Matthew 13:24-30).

3. Don't _____ anything without referring to the Bible.

4. Consider _____ and _____ events. For example, who were the Levites, Pharisees, Samaritans, etc.?

5. Learn when to stop interpreting. Don't _____. For example, Mark 12:3 states that the father believed that the tenants would respect his son, but this does not mean that the Father believed that the Jews would accept or respect His Son.

6. Preachers/Speakers might use or _____ the parable in a certain way to get their points across. Remember, the Holy Spirit can speak different messages to different people using the same parable.

7. We can _____ more than one spiritual meaning/interpretation from each parable.

8. We don't have to _____ every word mentioned in the parable. But God can shine a light on every word.

9. Do not build theological beliefs or denominational doctrines based _____ on a parable. Parables are intended to illustrate doctrine, not declare it. Do not build a whole doctrine on only one parable if

that message is not taught clearly elsewhere in the Bible. For example, teaching salvation by good works based on the parable of the sheep and goats alone would be dangerous because this doctrine is not clarified elsewhere in the Bible.

Conclusion:

❖ Don't think this Bible study is enough. Use it as a springboard to study more in depth on your own as well.

❖ Don't overlook or underestimate the parables. Parables are great treasures that help us in understanding God's mind.

❖ Comprehend the blessings and the grace of God that we were born in this day and age where the gospel, many insights, and scripture interpretations are at our disposal.

❖ The parables are copious tools for our faith walk. (Romans16:25-26)

Going forward each chapter will follow the format below:

I. **Bible Passage**

    a. **Reading**

    b. **Explanation of the Parable**

    c. **Cultural Relevance**

II. **Occasion/Reason why Jesus tells this Parable**

III. **Main Lessons (Thoughts) to Learn from the Parable**

IV. **Composition of the Parable**

V. **Discussion**

VI. **Conclusion**

VII. **Homework / Memory Verse**

VIII. **Middle-Eastern Recipe (make at home or for group study to share)**

CHAPTER 2

The Good Samaritan

Parables
DECODED
of Jesus

I. Bible Passage

a. Reading Luke 10:25-42

"²⁵ On one occasion an expert in the law stood up to test Jesus. "Teacher," he asked, "what must I do to inherit eternal life?" ²⁶ "What is written in the Law?" he replied. "How do you read it?" ²⁷ He answered: "'Love the Lord your God with all your heart and with all your soul and with all your strength and with all your mind'; and, 'Love your neighbor as yourself.' " [28] "You have answered correctly," Jesus replied. "Do this and you will live." [29] But he wanted to justify himself, so he asked Jesus, "And who is my neighbor?" [30] In reply Jesus said: "A man was going down from Jerusalem to Jericho, when he fell into the hands of robbers. [31] They stripped him of his clothes, beat him and went away, leaving him half dead. A priest happened to be going down the same road, and when he saw the man, he passed by on the other side. [32] So too, a Levite, when he came to the place and saw him, passed by on the other side. [33] But a Samaritan, as he traveled, came where the man was; and when he saw him, he took pity on him. [34] He went to him and bandaged his wounds, pouring on oil and wine. Then he put the man on his own donkey, took him to an inn and took care of him. [35] The next day he took out two silver coins and gave them to the innkeeper. 'Look after him,' he said, 'and when I return, I will reimburse you for any extra expense you may have.' [36] "Which of these three do you think was a neighbor to the man who fell into the hands of robbers?" [37] "The expert in the law replied, "The one who had mercy on him." Jesus told him, "Go and do likewise."

b. Explanation of the Parable

A traveler was robbed and left to die. Several prominent religious people left the man in peril. But a Samaritan, looked on by Jews as a despised subculture, stopped to help the man. He went so far as to take the wounded man to an inn. The Samaritan cared for the injured man and then left him in good care until the man healed. The expert had to admit anyone/everyone is our neighbor when confronted with Jesus's question. So we are commanded to love everyone as we love ourselves.

c. Cultural Relevance

History:

Samaritans and Jews were considered different races, nationalities, and religions. The enmity between Samaritans and Jews went back for centuries. Both believed in the _____ (first five books of the Old Testament) but Samaritans also worshiped idols. The final conflict that increased the hostility between them was about 6 B.C. when the Samaritans put unclean bones in the temple. From that time on, Jews determined that even mentioning the word "Samaritan" would deem them

_____.

Geography:

Jerusalem is about 17 miles from Jericho. Jerusalem was 3,300 feet higher (2/3 mile) in elevation than Jericho. So many ambushes and crimes occurred on the road from Jerusalem to Jericho that it was commonly referred to as *"The Path of Blood"*.

The Romans occupied the entire nation of Israel, but Greeks, and other nationalities lived in Israel as well. To the Jews, a neighbor was a family member and others of the

Jewish nationality. No other nations, including the Samaritans, were considered _____.

Did the expert in the law who questioned and then answered Jesus understand what was necessary to inherit eternal life? Did he summarize the law correctly?

_____

_____

_____

_____

"Love the Lord your God with all your heart and with all your soul and with all your strength." (Deuteronomy 6:5)

"Do not seek revenge or bear a grudge against one of your people, but love your neighbor as yourself. I am the Lord." (Leviticus 19:18)

The law and Jewish teaching were quite different from other common "eye for an eye" teachings of the day. Indeed, an Arab adage still widely quoted today in the Middle East says, "He who does not take revenge from the transgressor would better be dead than to walk without pride."

II.　　Occasion/Reason why Jesus Tells this Parable

The Jews believed they would _____eternal life because they were born into a Jewish family. But a lawyer (theologian/expert) stood up to test Jesus by asking Him what a man must do to inherit eternal life? Jesus asked what does the Law require? The lawyer replied you shall love the Lord your God with all your heart, all your soul, and all your mind. And, love your neighbor as yourself. Jesus replied, your answer is correct: Do that and you shall live. The expert in the law wanted to justify himself, so, he challenged Jesus on who his neighbor was.

_____

_____

_____

_____

III. Main Lessons (Thoughts) to Learn from the Parable

a. Eternal life is not inherited via earthly _____.

b. The Law can save you "**if** you can live it _____", which no human can.

c. Love means acting to meet a person's _____. But in God's sight, we have no valid reason for refusing to help someone.

d. We must help those in need _____of who they are.

e. Our _____is anyone of any race, creed, social background, or IQ who is in need. Even though we judge unworthy.

f. Lack of compassion is easy to _____, even though it is never right. Believers must be willing to get involved and meet needs.

g. Racism is not _____.

IV. Composition of the Parable

Some interpretations and representations that we have found:

a. "Down" from Jerusalem to Jericho represents not being in the right _____.

b. Thieves represent the enemy, _____.

c. Thieves taking everything represents the enemy _____ in life.

d. Life and death represent the results and outcome of _____.

e. Priests represent those whom you should expect to _____ the Word of God.

f. Levites represent religious people or _____.

g. Two pieces of silver represent paying the _____ to heal us.

h. Inn or hotel represents a temporary _____.

i. Oil represents the _____ of God.

j. Wine represents the _____ Spirit.

V. Discussion

The law requires us to "love" God with all our hearts. Grace showed that God has loved us with all His _____.

> Imagine if Jesus were to go to a cemetery and say to the dead people, "I'll raise anyone but ONLY if they raise their hand." Of course that doesn't make sense because if they raise their hand, then they don't need Jesus to resurrect them from death.

Similarly, Jesus said to the lawyer, "Do this and you will live," which means he was dead and needed to do something in order to live. But Jesus came to give us life and to fulfill the Law on our behalf.

The Law requires adherents love their neighbor as they love themselves. We are already guilty of not following that portion.

> Let's suppose a man was on his way back from work when he heard that his house was on fire and his wife and children were home. He began to panic at the news, running to get home. When he reached his street, he saw a heavy cloud of smoke but then realized it wasn't his house. It was the house next door. He took a deep breath and said,

"Thank God". According to the law, this man is guilty because he should have loved his neighbor as himself, showing exactly the same urgency, emotion and care for his neighbors as his own.

The law is hard to live, but if you are successful you will have eternal life. Jesus says do that "if you can" and you will live.

Those who are under the law must "**do**" in order to live. But to us who are free from the Law, Jesus said in John 5:24, "Very truly I tell you, whoever '**hears**' my word and believes him who sent me has eternal life and will not be judged but has crossed over from death to life."

Participants:

In this parable, we need to look at the _____ of each person to fully understand this familiar story that has become a part of our culture and vocabulary:

1. **The _____ (theologian)**: asks an errant question because:

o Earthly inheritance is not based on any work or achievement. Rather, it is bestowed simply for being a descendant.

- We don't do anything to be children of our parents. We inherit their looks, reputation, possessions, wealth, etc. If your father is a king, you automatically are royalty.

- He was a lawyer, an expert in the law, which means he had earned a level of high educational achievement to be able to answer such a question.

- He made himself sound humble and eager to learn, but really he was testing Jesus.

   2. **The** _____:

   a. We might assume that his misfortune was his fault for traveling "the Path of Blood". We might even blame him, thinking that he should have had a traveling companion.

   But many people fall into similar situations and they need a helping hand at times.

   b. Jesus purposely did not mention His nationality.

   The traveler was robbed, stripped and left to die. Jesus intentionally makes where the traveler comes from irrelevant. He wanted to let the lawyer (theologian) know that being a neighbor has nothing to do with nationalities.

   c. He was hurt, physically, emotionally, and spiritually.

d. He needed someone to care for and check on him.

3. The _____:

i. Just like Satan, the robbers lay waiting for their prey. They stole everything, clothes, wealth, and health.

ii. Everyone who doesn't know Christ is subject to losing everything as well, most importantly, eternal life.

4. The _____:

i. Every priest must be a Levite, but not every Levite was a priest.

ii. These highly regarded leaders interpreted the law and explained it thoroughly.

iii. They were also responsible for offering sacrifices for their own sins and the sins of others, as well as the caring for the temple.

5. _____:

i. This people group descended from the tribe of Levi.

ii. Their position was lower than priests but higher than the average Jewish citizen.

iii. They weren't allowed to offer sacrifices yet were responsible for safeguarding the Tabernacle and its utensils.

Let's consider this parable from the priest's and Levite's point of view. Could they have had good reasons for behaving the way they did?

If we bring this story up to more modern standards and imagine a priest or pastor of a congregation. He was on his way to preach to 200 people, but his car broke down so he had to walk the rest of the way to church. He is running late and doubtful he will make it on time. Then just past the coffee shop he sees a man who has been mugged alongside the road. The minister considers stopping but knows that 200 people will be waiting for him to preach, so he hurries on by. Is his behavior reasonable? Isn't nurturing 200 people a greater good than caring for just one?

If we want to continue the update, maybe the worship leader (the Levite) is a block behind the pastor. He's also in a hurry because he's late, so he walks on by the poor guy who was mugged. Reasonable?

The behavior of the pastor (priest) and worship leader (Levite) in the example above is not selfish or even uncaring. The problem is that Jesus emphasizes in His teachings that we are to care for the one sheep that got lost, not the 99 who didn't go astray, and in our example, the one person was hurt, not the 200 who were okay.

These are difficult lessons and following them may well put us in awkward or uncomfortable situations. It's easy for us to point fingers at the priest and Levite. But what would be our response?

_____

_____

_____

_____

_____

_____

The priest and the Levite showed no mercy or even took a minute to see if the man was alive.

According to the law, Leviticus 21:14 prohibited both Levites and priests from touching a dead person. If they touched a corpse, they would become unclean and would not be able to fulfill their religious duties for seven days (Numbers 19:11).

The Samaritan's Response:

Luke 10:33 says simply that the Samaritan took pity (or had compassion) on him. The Samaritan was not a friend or acquaintance of the man he helped. They didn't live on the same street or in the same city, so they were not physical neighbors. Moreover, they belong to peoples that are hostile to one another. Samaritans were considered "half- breeds," Jews who intermarried with their Assyrian conquerors in 740 B.C. and other invaders over the next centuries. Each group was zealous for his own faith and despised that of the other. The barriers between them were as strong and high as they could be.

Yet the natural pity and compassion of the Samaritan leapt over their differences. He saw the distressed man, not as a Jew or devotee of the temple in Jerusalem, but a needy man and brother. With generous humility, refusing to be hampered by artificial relations and the accidents of birth, residence, and creed, he bestowed upon the traveler his kindness and aid.

One might safely assume that traveling this route was a fairly regular practice of the Samaritan, as the inn keeper trusted him to settle his balance when he returned.

The good Samaritan is an example of Jesus Himself. When He saw us hurt, He was moved and filled with compassion.

Jesus clearly wants us to love everyone. He does not want us to love only those who love us or look like us. In Matthew 5:43, Jesus said, "You heard to love your neighbor and hate your enemy. But I say to you love your enemy."

Jesus made clear that the injured man had no money to pay back the Samaritan to show that the Samaritan acted from the kindness of his heart.

Jesus also showed that even the unclean Samaritan's actions exceeded the priest and the Levite. He illustrated that true love doesn't know race, nationality, or religion.

What was the Samaritan's response to the traveler? Why did he help the beaten man? How practical was his approach?

_____

_____

_____

Excuses:

Jesus knows our nature, that we always have a great excuse for our shortcomings. Here are some of the excuses the priest and the Levite might have come up with:

a. The _____man might be dead, causing me to be unclean (see Numbers 19:11-13).

b. I just finished my duty. I don't need to do more. Some treat church and ministry with a "clocked in/clocked out"

_____.

c. This might be a _____to rob me.

d. It might take too much _____to help him, and this could delay me from fulfilling my duty.

e. I don't have _____for this.

f. I might be _____of wounding the man.

g. I'll let someone _____help.

We all come up with excuses from time to time. Some are reasonable while others are short-fallen justifications or actions.

"If anyone, then, knows the good they ought to do and doesn't do it, it is sin for them." (James 4:17 NIV)

What are the greatest inconveniences (excuses) in your life? (Ones involving expenditures of your time? Of money? Emotional issues? Travel plans? Working with others?)

_____

Extraordinary measures taken by the Samaritan:

1. He felt _____ when he didn't have to be.
2. Nationality, religion, or race did not stop him from _____.
3. He didn't help to _____ himself or to repay a favor to someone.
4. The Samaritan took a possibly "costly risk" by spending _____ and helping a man that could easily die.
5. He helped without previous _____. He just rolled up his sleeves and helped.
6. The Samaritan made _____ for the needy man beyond the initial encounter.
7. He wasn't looking for recognition or _____.

What natural inclinations make it easier for you to act like the priest and the Levite rather than the Samaritan? How can that be different?

_____

_____

_____

_____

VI. Conclusion

a. God looks at **all** humans as brothers and sisters, so we must work together to help anyone in need. (Matthew 5:45)

b. God wants His unconditional love to show through us to all mankind. (Matthew 25:34-40)

c. We are not here in this country/state/town/and church as an accident or by luck. (Ephesians 2:10)

d. God wants us to be the salt and the light of the world. We cannot hide, be hidden, or avoid those in need. (Matthew 5:13-16)

e. Jesus wants us to love those He loves.

f. Jesus saved us, so now we should share the message with others. Jesus showed us mercy, so now we need to show mercy.

What did Jesus Do?

We had no hope, He became our hope.

We were hurt and left to die the eternal death. He died for us instead.

We couldn't live a holy life, so He anointed us with oil and filled us with wine and the Holy Spirit.

We were exhausted and He carried us through the journey.

We were in debt; He paid it all.

Satan stole from us; Jesus restores.

He is here to heal our wounds and take care of us.

He came just for you. Each of us is equally loved and important to God.

Notes:

_____

_____

_____

_____

We must keep in mind that our bodies are the temple of the Holy Spirit. And taking care of others in need is similar to taking care of the temple of the Holy Spirit. (Others are also the temple of the Holy Spirit.)

God said to love your neighbor as you love yourself, and our duties as children of God is to love our neighbor regardless of who they are, what they do, or look like. We should have compassion and feel pity for them. James said if you can do good and don't, it is a sin. Jesus makes one of the greatest statements to the lawyer and to us today, "Go and do likewise".

Finally, Jesus wants to remind us that He left us in an inn (a temporary home). This life is temporary. He will return to take us to the eternal home with Him in Heaven.

Notes:

_____

_____

_____

_____

_____

_____

_____

VII. Homework / Memory Verse

Matthew 25:24: "He will reply, 'Truly I tell you, whatever you did not do for one of the least of these, you did not do for me.'"

In what ways can you personally, or can we as Christians, be more like the Samaritan? Is this something to aspire to? Is this something God expects of you?

_____

_____

_____

_____

_____

_____

How does it feel when someone has mercy on you? How do you feel when you get in trouble because of your own unwise actions? How does mercy feel then?

_____

_____

_____

_____

Prayer:

From your heart, pray David's prayer in Psalm 139:23-24, *"Search me, O God, and know my heart: try me, and know my thoughts. And see if there be any wicked way in me, and lead me in the way everlasting."*

VIII. Middle-Eastern Recipe

Rice Pudding *(Ruz bil Labn)*

Rice Pudding is a common Egyptian dessert. Sweet and creamy, it is a satisfying end to any meal. Traditionally, it is offered with tea or Turkish coffee.

INGREDIENTS:

- 1 cup short grain rice, uncooked
- 1 1/2 cups water
- 4 1/2 cups whole milk
- 1 1/2 cups sugar
- 1 teaspoon vanilla extract
- raisins, slivered almonds, shredded coconut for garnish

METHOD

Bring rice, water and milk to a boil in a large pot, watching that it doesn't boil over. Stir in the sugar. Reduce heat to low and stir frequently, careful it doesn't burn. Cook until the milk is absorbed and the pudding is thick and creamy approximately 1 hour. Add vanilla extract, taste, and add more sugar if desired. Remove from heat and cool for about 1 hour. Pour the pudding into individual ramekins, cover the surface of the pudding with plastic wrap, and refrigerate for at least another hour. Enjoy.

CHAPTER 3

The Fig Tree

Parables DECODED Of Jesus

I. Bible Passage

a. Reading Luke 13:6-9 NKJV

Fig Tree

"⁶ He also spoke this parable: "A certain man had a fig tree planted in his vineyard, and he came seeking fruit on it and found

none. ⁷ Then he said to the keeper of his vineyard, 'Look, for three years I have come seeking fruit on this fig tree and find none. Cut it down; why does it use up the ground?' ⁸ But he answered and

said to him, 'Sir, let it alone this year also, until I dig around it and fertilize it. ⁹ And if it bears fruit, well. But if not, after that you can cut it down.'"

b. Explanation of the parable

A fig tree grew in a vineyard, and didn't produce fruit for three years. The owner asked the gardener why the tree still stood. He thought the fig tree was useless and took nutrients from the vines. The gardener suggested that they keep it for another year. During that time, the gardener would clean around the fig tree and fertilize it. If the tree produced fruit, the owner would benefit. If not, the gardener would cut down the tree.

c. Cultural Relevance

1. You may be wondering why a fig tree was planted in a

_____.

In biblical times, fig trees often grew in vineyards.

- *"The vine has dried up, And the fig tree has withered."* Joel 1:12 (NKJV)
- *"The fig tree and the vine yield their strength."*

Joel 2:22 (NKJV)

Figs, along with grapes, have grown in Israel since ancient times; they served as tree stands letting the grape vines grow entwined on them. The tree was expected to be fruitful, especially because it was planted in the good earth of the vineyard. Yet the fig tree remained fruitless for years.

2. Historically, Galileans were _____. They rose against the Roman rule, and many of the revolts against the Roman government came from the area of Galilee. So the crowd was relaying to Jesus that some Galileans were probably involved in a ruckus against Rome. When Herod sent his soldiers, they found the Galileans offering sacrifices to God. So the soldiers killed them right there, mingling their blood with the blood of the sacrifices. Of course, to the Jews that was heinous.

3. The pool of Siloam was _____ because it was a main water supply for Jerusalem. Women washed clothes there. A tower was being built by the pool of Siloam and it fell, crushing eighteen people to death.

4. In the Jewish culture, health and _____ was a sign of God's blessing.

5. In the same way, poverty and _____ were signs that one was sinful and disobeying God.

Notes:

_____

_____

_____

_____

_____

_____

_____

_____

_____

_____

II. Occasion/Reason why Jesus tells this parable:

Just before this parable, Jesus said, "I tell you, no; but unless all repent, you will all likewise perish," (Luke 13:5 NKJV). In other words, this parable is given in the context of "the judgment of God." When we compare the judgment of God with the words of this vineyard owner, "Better chop it down!" has a very strict ring to them. We imagine a cold blooded and ruthless man. We compare that with the image of an angry God handing down His judgments in a pitiless manner. I'd say more than a few felt resistance to the words of the owner. But we must consider the parable in its context and entirety. What is being conveyed is contrary to a harsh master.

    a. Jesus told this parable _____ He received the news about what Pilate did to the Galileans.

    "There were present at that season some who told Him about the Galileans whose blood Pilate had mingled with their sacrifices." (Luke 13:1)

    b. Jesus was answering with a _____ saying unto them:

    "Do you suppose that these Galileans were sinners greater than all of the rest of the Galileans? Because they suffered such things?" (Luke 13:2)

    c. Jesus gets away from the question 'Why did this happen?' and _____it into, 'What does this mean to me?'

Do you think that this is an act of God's judgment because they were worse sinners than all the rest?

_____

_____

_____

III. Main lessons (Thoughts) to Learn from the parable

a. God judges based on the _____ we bear. God always looks for fruit from believers.

b. The _____ behind the judgment. Fruit trees that don't bear fruit are worthless.

c. The reason for _____, to repent.

d. Not to _____ others if they go through trials.

Too often something sad or tragic happens to a person, people think the event is judgment. "Oh, they are getting what they deserve, aren't they? I wonder what they did to deserve that terrible thing." Jesus corrects them. "Hey, do you think because this happened to them, they were worse sinners than the rest of the people in Galilee?" He said, "No way, and, unless you repent, you also are going to perish. Do you think the tower of Siloam fell on the eighteen people because they were worse sinners than the rest? (paraphrased Luke 13:3-4)

e. _____ good and bad things happen to everyone.

We normally think of some people as "good," and some people as "bad." We believe God should allow only good things to happen to good people and bad things to bad people. Jesus dispels this notion.

    f. Unless you _____, you likewise will perish: In analyzing the issue, Jesus got away from the question, "Why did this happen?" and turned it into, "What does this mean to me?"

IV. Composition of the parable

    a. Vineyard Owner: _____

    b. Gardener: _____

    c. Vineyard:

       1. The _____ (The People)

       2. The body of Christ

    d. _____ Tree:

       1. Nation of Israel (God's people)

       2. Human efforts

       (Another interpretation can be that our human nature and efforts do not work in the body of Christ because

He is the one who brings forth the fruit.)

    e. Years: Period of _____

    f. Dig and fertilize: Clean with the _____ of God and the Cross

    g. _____: Fruit of ministry or Fruit of the Spirit

_____

_____

_____

_____

_____

V. Discussion

The tree in this story does not yield fruit even though it was at fruit bearing age. Years go by and it doesn't have fruit. According to the law of Moses even if a tree has fruit, it can't be eaten right away. It can't be eaten for three years. The fruit from the fourth year will be an offering to the Lord. Then after the fifth year it can be eaten. So, even had it yielded on the third year, the fruit would be edible in the forth year. No fruit had come at its third year considering that, it's not odd for the fig tree to be judged useless and unfit. "Chop it down" is a reasonable judgment. Even if some felt resistance to the owner in some way or another, we'd probably be the first to say, "Chop it down" if we had been in his shoes. That much, in a sense, would have been within our rights as an owner.

The fig tree was not growing wild along the side of the road. The tree had been planted in the good soil of the vineyard with a gardener to care for the plants. When we consider the Old Testament background to this parable, figs are not trees that have been turned wild. The culture assumes that the tree has been tended to by hand. In other words, despite all that, after three years no fruit had ever been found on it. Once again, to say "chop it down" is an altogether practical judgment call.

So, we need to take another look at this passage to determine what it says about God's judgment. Most often we resist depictions of God's wrath. We feel a resistance to the harsh words of the owner in this parable. But the truly important thing is that we admit that by our very natures we exist as helpless to being judged. Even if God judged and destroyed the world, it would not be an immoral or an abnormal act. It is within God's sovereign right as King of the universe.

When you understand this, the especially surprising thing being said in this parable is not in the first half but rather in the second part, the patience of the gardener.

This parable is given in the context of "God's judgment." When we think of God's judgment, our thoughts inevitably turn to whether we will be chopped down or saved on "the last day." However, the parable of the fig tree draws our eyes to turn "the last day" back to "now, this hour," in which we stand under the intercession of Christ and are shown God's mercy and patience.

The gardener asked that the fruitless fig tree might stay on till next year. Were the tree to remain, the gardener would gain no benefit. Instead, it would only add the extra workload of the gardener digging around the tree and giving it fertilizer.

Nevertheless, the gardener petitioned the owner on behalf of the tree. The parable ends with the gardener's words. In the final analysis, the message to be implied by that is that the owner did not reject the gardener's words. This response is not what you'd expect, and it is rather surprising.

We must respond with gravity in this hour given to us as a gift of grace for now, for this very present moment. Paul said, "Right now is the hour of grace; right now is the day of salvation" (2 Corinthians 6:2).

Some facts about fig trees.

    i. The fig tree is the _____ tree mentioned in the Bible. Tree of life, tree of Knowledge, and then the fig tree.

"Then the eyes of both of them were opened, and they knew that they were naked; and they sewed fig leaves together and made themselves coverings." Genesis 3:7 (NKJV)

    ii. _____ fig trees will not produce fruit for the first four-five years.

    iii. Fig trees give _____ harvests per year. The first harvest occurs in June and the second in August.

    iv. The _____ harvest is called "Breba Crop". The fruit is small, acidic and inferior in texture, but it can be preserved.

    v. The _____ harvest is stronger and superior in both quantity and quality.

    vi. Figs _____ from the inside, not the outside. It's the tiny flowers that produce the crunchy sound.

    vii. Fruit appears (grows) _____ or at the same time as leaves appear on the tree. Leaves fall about December.

    viii. The fig tree is a symbol of _____ and safety to the nation of Israel (see 1 Kings 4:25).

ix.   The fig tree _____ the nation of Israel.

The Lord desires to receive fruit and is not. He is coming for fruit from His chosen people and not finding it. Yet He gives another opportunity to bear fruit. Believers who don't produce fruit bear consequences.

A. Invitation to repent

Jesus's answer reveals the following:

i.   Problems and trials are not necessarily a result of _____. The killing of those Galilean men didn't mean they were worse than other Galileans.

"And Jesus answered and said to them, "Do you suppose that these Galileans were worse sinners than all other Galileans, because they suffered such things?" (Luke 13:2)

ii.   Problems and trials _____ be a result of sin.

"I tell you, no; but unless you repent you will all likewise perish." (Luke 13:3)

iii.   Jesus made clear that trials come on _____ righteous people and sinners. Jesus refers historically to when the tower of Siloam fell on eighteen people.

iv. Everything going well doesn't necessarily mean that God is _____. We see sinners looking good, happy, rich, famous, etc.. Just as the sun shines on both and it rains on both. Trials and goodness happen to both the sinners and the righteous.

v. The Lord sometimes _____ trials to lead us to repentance, not just for sinners to repent but for all to repent.

vi. God sends trials to whomever he wants, but we need to be reminded to _____ when we see others going through trials.

B. Invitation to be fruitful

i. Fig trees are unique in that both mature leaves and ripe fruit appear at the same time. Therefore if you see leaves, you expect fruit! (You can refer to Matt 21, Jesus cursing the fig tree). A fig tree with mature leaves and no fruit symbolizes _____.

ii. In addition to symbolizing the nation of Israel, the fig tree also can symbolize each _____ as well. Just as a fig tree must be fruitful, each of us must be fruitful.

iii. _____fig trees with leaves symbolizes living by works not by faith, or trying to do good deeds or good works to purify ourselves. Only the gardener (Jesus) can clean and purify us.

iv. Just as a fig tree with leaves and no fruit symbolizes our human efforts, Adam and Eve try to cover their shame with leaves without the true cure (salvation). But Jesus came to correct our ruined _____if we accept Him.

C. **Invitation to use the advocate (Jesus)**

Just as the government in the United States issues a free lawyer if you cannot afford one, God issues a free "lawyer" because He knew we could not possibly "afford" an eternal one.

   i. Jesus is our _____.

"My little children, these things write I unto you, that ye sin not. And if any man sin, we have an advocate with the Father, Jesus Christ the righteous." (1 John 2:1 KJV)

   ii. We should look no further than the one and only advocate – _____.

"For there is one God, and one mediator between God and men, the man Christ Jesus." (1 Timothy 2:5)

   iii. Jesus is always _____for us. He will always intercede on behalf of believers.

"But he answered and said to him, 'Sir, let it alone this year also, until I dig around it and fertilize it. And if it bears fruit, well. But if not, after that you can cut it down." (Luke 13:8 -9)

This might be the most important question in your life... What season of life am I in?

_____

_____

_____

_____

Life Application:

1. Which is most surprising to you: That the owner wants to cut down the tree? Or that the gardener wants to give it another year?

_____

_____

_____

_____

_____

2. What is the message this parable brings? How can you apply it to your life?

_____

_____

_____

_____

_____

_____

VI.   Conclusion

We clearly see in this parable justice and mercy meeting.

Verse 7: Cut it down; why does it use up the ground? Verse 8: Let it alone this year also, until I dig around it and fertilize it.

We also clearly see the special care Jesus has for each one of us.

The gardener took care of the fig tree that needed help most. God always gives us special care. Leaving all the other trees and taking care of the one… leaving all the sheep and looking for the lost one, leaving nine coins and looking for the lost one, looking and waiting for the lost son. Over and over He demonstrates the value of the one.

He gives us enough chances just like He gave the tree another year, that included summer, fall, winter, and spring, as well as rain, wind, sun, soil, and fertilizer, and special attention.

Don't take advantage of God's patience like the foolish do.

By noting the ancient Greek grammar, we see that Jesus mentioned two kinds of repentance, and both are essential. In Luke 13:5, "unless you repent" describes a "once and for all" repentance. The verb tense in Luke 13:3, "unless you repent" describes continuing repentance.

Repentance must be a top priority. Those who died in both instances before the parable is recorded did not think they would die soon, but they did. We can suppose most of them were not ready.

What fruit is God looking for? It certainly has to begin with the fruit of the Spirit, mentioned in Galatians 5:22-23, *"But the fruit of the Spirit is love, joy, peace, longsuffering, kindness, goodness, faithfulness, gentleness, self-control."*

_____

_____

_____

_____

VII. Homework / Memory Verse

Let the Holy Spirit search your heart. Repent for any sin, hidden or visible.

Dear Lord, thank you that you are patient with me and Your desire is that none perish. Thank you for sending your son Jesus to die in my place. I accept His willing sacrifice and receive your forgiveness of all my sins. Lead my life, guide me in your paths I pray. In Jesus's name, Amen.

Notes:

_____

_____

_____

_____

_____

VIII. Middle-Eastern Recipe

Fig Jam

(Yield: about 1 pint)

A simple yet tasty recipe that makes an elegant addition to a cheese plate or a sweet breakfast treat. Eat it by the spoonful or scoop it up with some pita bread. It's delicious!

INGREDIENTS:

1 cup sugar

½ cup water

Juice of 1 lemon

3 cups coarsely chopped dried figs

1 cup chopped walnuts, toasted

2-3 teaspoons aniseed or cardamom (optional)

METHOD

In a saucepan, combine the sugar, water, and lemon juice.

Bring the mixture up to a boil and reduce heat to simmer, stirring frequently for 20 to 30 minutes until thickened and slightly syrupy. Pay attention to the jam stirring so it doesn't stick or scorch.

Remove the fig mixture from the heat and stir in the chopped nuts and aniseed or cardamom as desired.

Cool and store in jars. Store in the refrigerator and eat within the month. Enjoy!

CHAPTER 4

Workers in the Vineyard

Parables
dEC0ƎD
Of Jesus

I. Bible Passage

a. Reading Matthew 20:1-16

1 "For the kingdom of heaven is like a landowner who went out early in the morning to hire laborers for his vineyard. **2** Now when he had agreed with the laborers for a denarius a day, he sent them into his vineyard. **3** And he went out about the third hour and saw others standing idle in the marketplace, **4** and said to them, 'You also go into the vineyard, and whatever is right I will give you.' So they went. **5** Again he went out about the sixth and the ninth hour, and did likewise. **6** And about the eleventh hour he went out and found others standing idle, and said to them, 'Why have you been standing here idle all day?' **7** They said to him, 'Because no one hired us.' He said to them, 'You also go into the vineyard, and whatever is right you will receive.' **8** So when evening had come, the owner of the vineyard said to his steward, 'Call the laborers and give them their wages, beginning with the last to the first.' **9** And when those came who were hired about the eleventh hour, they each received a denarius. **10** But when the first came, they supposed that they would receive more; and they likewise received each a denarius. **11** And when they had received it, they complained against the landowner, **12** saying, 'These last men have worked only one hour, and you made them equal to us who have borne the burden and the heat of the day.' **13** But he answered one of them and said, 'Friend, I am doing you no wrong. Did you not agree with me for a denarius? **14** Take what is yours and go your way. I wish to give to this last man the same as to you. **15** Is it not lawful for me to do what I wish with my own things? Or is your eye evil because I am good?' **16** So the last will be first, and the first last. For many are called, but few chosen."

b. Explanation of the Parable

The Kingdom of heaven is like the owner of a vineyard who hired workers throughout the day to work his land. He hired the first group in the morning to work for one denarius for the day. He hired additional laborers throughout the day. He instructed the foreman to pay the last hired workers first and pay each a denarius. When the turn of those who came in the first hour to get paid came, they expected to get paid more, but they also earned one denarius. They complained that those who worked one hour received the same pay those who worked all day with burden and the heat of the day. The owner asked, "Do you think I'm not fair to you? Didn't we agree that you work one day for a denarius and I'm giving you what we agreed on?" He sent the first laborers away, explaining that he wanted to give those who came last the same as the first. The owner asked if he had the right to do what he wanted with his money. Then he asked if the workers were jealous because of his generosity. "So the last will be first, and the first will be last," Jesus concluded.

c. Cultural Relevance

Men who didn't have an occupation, steady job, or trade used to stand in the marketplace waiting for someone to hire them for an agreed-on amount, similar to freelance workers today. Those men were hired to do anything the hirer needed them to do, for example clean up, dig holes, etc. They usually got hired for a job that could take a day or several days, but it wasn't a permanent job. Of course, depending on the employer, the job could turn into what we call today a full or part-time job.

Let's look briefly at the culture of Jesus's time and some common principles of the Jews:

a) If you keep the law, you _____ go to Heaven.

b) If you look good from the _____, you must be a good person.

c) If you are _____, you must be good.

"It is easier for a camel to get through the eye of a needle than for a rich man to enter the kingdom." The disciples ask "then who can be saved?" (Matthew 19:24).

d) Two chapters earlier, in Matthew 18, we read about the Pharisee and the tax collector. We learned that our actions cannot _____us in God's eyes. In this parable, Jesus wants to make it even clearer.

Does this parable make sound economic sense? Does it in any way fit with unions, employers, and government guidelines in the world we live in? How do our cultural values struggle with the idea of grace?

_____

_____

_____

Jesus's story does not make financial sense, and that was His intent. His illustration does not in any way fit with today's systems. Jesus was giving us a parable about grace, which cannot be calculated like a day's wages. No one was cheated; all the workers got what they were promised. But discontentment arises from the scandalous mathematics of grace.

Jesus says right at the start, this parable is about the Kingdom of Heaven. As such, it points to a great truth: Many who were called last will be first in the Kingdom of Heaven, while the first called will be last. Our reward in Christ's kingdom will not depend solely on the greatness, our fatigue, and length of our work but above all on the grace and favor of God.

II. Occasion/Reason why Jesus tells this Parable

Matthew 19:16-30 "Now behold, one came and said to Him, "Good Teacher, what good thing shall I do that I may have eternal life?" **17** So He said to him, "Why do you call Me good? No one is good but One, that is, God. But if you want to enter into life, keep the commandments." **18** He said to Him, "Which ones?" Jesus said, "'You shall not murder,' 'You shall not commit adultery,' 'You shall not steal,' 'You shall not bear false witness,' **19** 'Honor your father and your mother,' and, 'You shall love your neighbor as yourself.' " **20** The young man said to Him, "All these things I have kept from my youth. What do I still lack?" **21** Jesus said to him, "If you want to be perfect, go, sell what you have and give to the poor, and you will have treasure in heaven; and come, follow Me." **22** But when the young man heard that saying, he went away sorrowful, for he had great possessions. **23** Then Jesus said to His disciples, "Assuredly, I say to you that it is hard for a rich man to enter the kingdom of heaven. **24** And again I say to you, it is easier for a camel to go through the eye of a needle than for a rich man to enter the kingdom of God." **25** When His disciples heard it, they were greatly astonished, saying, "Who then can be saved?" **26** But Jesus looked at them and said to them, "With men this is impossible, but with God all things are possible." **27** Then Peter answered and said to Him, "See, we have left all and followed You. Therefore what shall we have?" **28** So Jesus said to them, "Assuredly I say to you, that in the regeneration, when the Son of Man sits on the throne of His glory, you who have followed Me will also sit on twelve thrones, judging the twelve tribes of Israel. **29** And everyone who has left houses or brothers or sisters or father or mother or wife or children or lands, for My name's sake, shall receive a hundredfold, and inherit eternal life. **30** But many who are first will be last, and the last first."

a) Jesus asked, "Why do you call me good? No one is good but One, and that's God."

b) Needle's-Eye was a small gate next a big gate in Jerusalem.

III. Main Lessons (Thoughts) to Learn from the Parable

    a. _____is for all by grace – Jew or Gentile – at any age – and not by works.

    b. _____is an open invitation for all to serve – and the reward is for everyone.

    c. We are not to grumble or _____.

    d. We must focus on working _____for our Lord and let Him worry about the reward.

    e. What seems _____to us could be perfect justice in God's eyes.

IV.   Composition of the Parable:

  1. Landowner = _____

  2. Landowner **went out** = God didn't _____ for sinners to come to Him, instead; He came to invite them

  3. _____of the day = two meanings:

      i. human life OR

      ii. generations

4. _____= rewards for Christian believers – Heaven – it is a gift from God because "He is good" and has NOTHING to do with our works but reflects God's generosity

5. Market = the _____

6. Standing idle = those who have not accepted _____ as Savior

7. Vineyard = the ministry _____to bring harvest to the body of Christ

8. Grumbling or complaining = Hebrews complained as other tribes were accepted and received _____

9. Do what I wish with my own things = Salvation _____ to the Lord

_____

_____

_____

_____

_____

V. Discussion

Before we continue, we need to have a clear understanding about what Jesus said to the rich man. "Why do you ask me about what is good?" Jesus replied. "There is only One who is good" (Matthew 19:17). Some think that Jesus is proclaiming He is not God. In fact, Jesus is actually proclaiming that He is. Jesus did not say "Don't call me good". Instead, Jesus asked a question, "Why do you call me good; there is no one good but God". As if Jesus is asking the man, "Did you finally believe that I'm God? And that's why you are calling me good?"

What wage was agreed upon by the landowner and workers early in the morning? (Verse 20:2) What wage was agreed upon by those hired later? (Verse 20:4)

_____

_____

A full day's labor at harvest time was about twelve hours. The landowner's own workers would have started work at 6:00 a.m. Three hours later, the landowner saw that he needed more workers and hired some at 9:00 a.m., who would know that they had to work nine hours to earn a denarius, a fair wage for a full day's labor. The owner then hired more laborers at noon, 3:00 p.m., and finally at 5:00 p.m. to help finish. To the workers hired later on, the employer didn't state a wage, but said he would pay "whatever is right."

Understanding "Hours" according to the Hebrew clock.
(Note: Workday was 12 hours)

Hebrew Standard Time	Today Eastern Standard Time.
First hour	6AM
3rd Hour	9AM
6th Hour	12PM
11th Hour	5PM
12th Hour (end of Work Day)	6PM

If the first man is going to get one denarius for twelve hours' work, what do you expect the second group to get? Three-quarters, then 1/2 then 1/4 and then 1/12th respectively?

The landowner went to pay everyone starting with the last group. He gave them each 1 denarius. That's one denarius/hour. What do you expect the next group to get? Three denarii. The next group six, and the next nine and the first group that was hired should expect to get 12 denarii.

The landowner made an agreement only with the first group, everyone else was hired later, and he never made a deal with them concerning the pay. But everyone received what they expected or deserved. This is the same principal of justice and grace.

" I must work the works of Him who sent Me while it is day; the night is coming when no one can work. ⁵ As long as I am in the world, I am the light of the world." (John 9:4-5)

God's voice calls to us all of our lives here on earth. The implication is you must work and don't delay as long as there is day.

You might think, there were some people who stayed till the eleventh hour.

BUT… Please note:

1. The workers who began at 5:00 p.m. weren't _____ work. No one had hired them. The True Word of God hadn't reached them yet. They wanted

to work. They **weren't** lazy or waiting until the eleventh hour.

2. God didn't _____ for sinners to become righteous; instead, He came for them.

Entry to Heaven is NOT based on what we deserve but on grace and the Blood of Jesus

What did the landowner tell the foreman to do at the end of the day? (Verse 20:8)

_____

_____

_____

Salvation is for everyone

1. The master didn't just _____ certain people. He invited everyone who was looking for work.

2. The master went out to the streets calling those who have NO _____ to work and offered them a job with pay.

3. The meaning of the workday is open to _____:

- If you feel God's voice saying that the "day" means generations, then God is calling our generation to work in His field.
- If you feel God's voice saying that the "day" means human life, then God is calling you at every phase and age you are in.

The Jews had been "working" for God for more than 2,000 years already, and it did not seem right that God would let Gentiles in at such a late hour and give them all the blessings of the kingdom.

What explanation did the last group of workers give when asked why they were standing around doing nothing? How do you see this applying to yourself or others today?

_____

_____

_____

Don't Delay

"It is good for a man to bear the yoke in his youth." (Lamentations 3:27)

"Remember now your Creator in the days of your youth, Before the difficult days come, And the years draw near when you say," I have no pleasure in them." (Ecclesiastes 12:1)

Equal Opportunity Reward

"Even when we were dead in trespasses, made us alive together with Christ (by grace you have been saved)." (Ephesians 2:5, emphasis added)

"For by grace you have been saved through faith, and that not of yourselves; it is the gift of God" (Ephesians 2:8)

The master said "whatever is right," meaning "whatever is rightfully yours". ALL will receive eternal life, but each will earn different crowns.

Accept Ministry (Serving)

1. We are _____ indebted to our Savior for paying a price we could never pay. Therefore, we should not look or wait for a reward or pay. But God is generous; he will reward us with eternal life.
2. People who are _____ in their own eyes are _____ in God's eyes. And others who are last in people's eyes are first in God's eyes.

For example, the Israelites were first to be called of God but last to answer the calling, while the Gentiles were last to receive the calling but were first to answer it.

"Which of the two did the will of his father?" They said to Him, "The first." Jesus said to them, "Assuredly, I say to you that tax collectors and harlots enter the kingdom of God before you." (Matthew 21:31)

Complaining Workers:

The workers who worked longest thought they were better. So they complained about those who came later to accept the call. The Jews who complained where just like the older son who complained when the younger son returned in the parable of the prodigal son. Perhaps, they were full of envy, because they didn't lose anything. They received what they had agreed upon, but they were angry that others received something better.

Was anyone underpaid or cheated? Why then did the workers complain? Was anyone overpaid?

_____

_____

_____

Observe that nobody was cheated! Not a single worker was underpaid. While it can be argued (based on human, subjective, economic comparisons) that some were overpaid, nobody was cheated. The complaint of the early workers offered no evidence of wrongdoing. But their complaint wasn't unjustified either. Theirs was a complaint born in hearts of jealousy, not objective reality. The early hires received less than they expected but the many later hires received more. We should rejoice in the good others receive. But do we?

The landowner had the right to "overpay" the late workers. He said "whatever is right you will receive." He determined what was right, not based on ordinary human accounting, but grace. His overpayment of the late workers was his choice and nobody could argue he didn't have that right.

Question

Why are you standing and "not working"? Take a moment to answer:

_____

_____

The Lord wants you to serve Him with:

1. Your _____
2. Your _____
3. Your _____
4. _____ you have

Don't wait to be:

1. _____ by someone
2. _____ of serving God
3. _____ enough
4. _____ enough
5. _____ enough

What would happen if God gave each of us what we deserve?

_____

_____

As stated above, God doesn't reward us according to merit—thank goodness—for we just don't come close to meeting God's requirements for a perfect life. If we were paid on the basis of our works, we would all end up in hell.

Notes:

_____

_____

_____

_____

_____

_____

10. Conclusion

"Do you not say, 'There are still four months and then comes the harvest?' Behold, I say to you, lift up your eyes and look at the fields, for they are already white for harvest!" (John 4:35-36)

"I must work the works of Him who sent Me while it is day; the night is coming when no one can work." (John 9:4)

- Jesus ends the parable with this proverb—"the last shall be first and the first last," which means if you are striving to be first, you won't make it.

- Whether you come in early or late, you can still enter and enjoy the benefits of God's Kingdom.

- Let's trust God's judgment.

- God is Sovereign, a Supreme Ruler. He chose us while He could have chosen others instead. Just as He chose Jacob over first-born Esau.

- God is generous. That should eliminate pride. If one person has more than another, that doesn't necessarily mean they each deserve what they have.

- How would you like to work for someone who was always fair, always in control, and generous to boot? Guess what—We do!

Question

Did the disciples learn the important lesson from this parable?

What's the danger of thinking of yourself as a responsible worker, hired early in the day? Why is it dangerous to compare your own situation with someone else's?

Significantly, many Christians who study this parable identify with the employees who put in a full day's work, rather than the add-ons at the end of the day. We like to think of ourselves as responsible workers, and the employer's strange behavior baffles us as it did the original hearers. We risk missing the point of the parable, that God dispenses gifts, not wages. None of us gets paid according to merit, for none of us comes close to fulfilling God's requirements for a perfect life. If paid on the basis of justice, we would all end up in hell.

Think of what this means today. We are called by God at

different hours of the day, that is, at different times in our lives, to His service. Look at people in the Bible. Some were called at birth like Samuel, Isaac, and Jacob; some were called while they were young like Joseph, David, and Solomon; others were called in their middle years like Noah and Jonah; and still others not until they were much older. So it is with us.

Some commentators add that another purpose of this parable is to stir zeal and encourage those who come (or return) to God in old age to realize they would not have any reason to expect less than those who started young. You can gain everything, even in a short time. Everyone can attain the same result at any age.

And, or course, this parable like so much of Jesus's teaching, emphasizes humility.

VII. Homework

If you accepted the invitation, you are invited to go invite others. The simplest words can bring the biggest harvest. Go and tell others about Jesus; become a servant.

1. What do you think of conversions to faith in Jesus that come last minute (like on someone's deathbed or a convict on death row)?

_____

2. With which group of workers do you personally identify—with those hired at 9:00 a.m., noon, 3:00 p.m., or those hired at 5:00 p.m.?

_____

3. How can focusing on God's grace in our lives keep us from becoming jealous of others? In what way can you thank God every day for his grace in your life?

_____

_____

Notes:

_____

_____

_____

_____

_____

_____

VIII. Middle-Eastern Recipe

Stuffed Grape Leaves

Vegetarian grape leaves are a staple among Middle-Eastern Christians (especially Coptic Orthodox Christians) who fast meat for many months of the year. It is a satisfying and delectable dish that has been adapted by many countries in the region.

INGREDIENTS

- 1 jar of grape leaves
- 2 medium sized onions finely chopped
- 1 can tomato paste (6 ounces)
- 1 bunch of Italian parsley finely chopped (cut off stems)
- ½ bunch of finely chopped dill
- ¼ bunch of cilantro finely chopped

- 2 tablespoons cumin
- 1 tablespoon pepper
- 1 tablespoon salt
- 1 cup of rice
- ¼ cup of clarified (or melted) butter
- 1 sliced medium onion
- 1 sliced medium tomato
- ½ cup olive oil

METHOD

Grape Leaves Stuffing Preparation

1. Sauté finely chopped onions in 1 tablespoon of oil until lightly browned.
2. In a bowl mix tomato paste, 2 ½ cups water, cooled sautéed onion, cilantro, Italian parsley (with stems removed), dill, rice, cumin, salt, pepper, melted butter, and rice.

Preparing the Leaves

1. Drain the jar of grape leaves and soak leaves in clean hot water for 3 to 4 minutes. Rinse leaves multiple times with fresh water to get rid of any preservatives.
2. Cut off their stems and stack them on a cutting board.

How to Roll the Grape Leaves

1. Lay the leaves flat on a cutting board with the rough side facing upwards.
2. Add ¾ teaspoon of stuffing towards the bottom of the leaf.

3. Roll the bottom of leaf over the stuffing a third of the way up.

4. Fold right side over one-third of the way.

5. Fold left side over one-third of the way.

6. Then roll all the way through the end of the leaf.

7. A good roll needs to be tight so that it doesn't break apart during cooking. We like to make medium to small rolls, about ½ inch thick and 3 inches long.

8. Once rolled, stack the grape leave rolls tightly in a pot with its bottom covered with a layer of sliced onions and a layer of sliced tomatoes.

Cooking the Grape Leaves

1. Once you've finished adding the rolls, sprinkle 1 teaspoon of salt on top, add ½ cup of olive oil, 2 cups of water.

2. Shake the pot sideways to let the liquids seep all the way through the bottom. The liquid should top the grape leave rolls.

3. Add a small (heat-safe) plate on top and press it downwards and leave in pot while cooking. The plate creates a downward pressure on the grape leave rolls to keep them tightly held together.

4. Cover the pot and cook for a few minutes on high heat until the sauce boils, then turn heat down to low and let simmer and cook for about 35 minutes.

5. Every 10 minutes or so, shake the pot slowly to ensure that the sauce is equally dispersed.

Serving and Tips

1. Once cooked uncover pot and let rest for about ½ hour to cool. During this time the grape leave rolls will absorb more sauce and enhance in flavor.

2. Once ready to serve, empty the sauce from the pot in a separate container, then put your serving plate upside down on top of the cooking pot, and while holding them tightly together turn them over quickly so the pot is now on top and the serving plate on the bottom.

3. Lay serving plate on the kitchen counter and slowly lift up and remove the pot from the plate. You should now have a nice looking pile of neatly stacked grape leave rolls with the tomatoes and onions on top. You can then add a bit of its sauce on it to taste.

CHAPTER 5

The Patch and the Wineskin

I. Bible Passage

    a.   **Reading Matthew 9:14-17; Mark 2:18-22; Luke 5:36-39**

Luke 5:36-39: ³⁶Then He spoke a parable to them. "No one puts a piece from a new garment on an old one; otherwise the new makes a tear, and also the piece that was taken out of the new does not match the old. ³⁷And no one puts new wine into old wineskins; or else the new wine will burst the wineskins and be spilled, and the wineskins will be ruined. ³⁸But new wine must be put into new wineskins, and both are preserved. ³⁹And no one, having drunk old wine, immediately desires new; for he says, 'The old is better.'"

b. Explanation of the Parable

Jesus illustrated His answer to the Pharisee with a parable. No one cuts a piece of cloth from a new shirt to fix a rip in an old shirt because that will end up ruining the new one and not repairing the old one either; both will be ruined. Jesus continued that no one puts new wine in an old wineskin (wine container) because the new wine will break the wineskin and spill onto the floor; both the new wine and the container will be ruined. Finally, Jesus said that when drinking old wine, no one desires new wine because the older wine always tastes better.

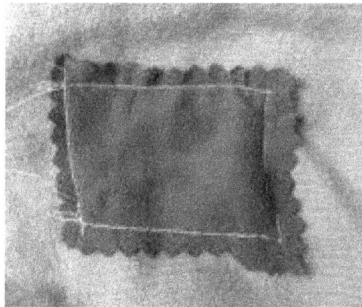

This parable was chronicled _____ times in the New Testament. That is why we mentioned all three accounts in the beginning of the study. This parable challenges us to _____ _____ about why we do what we do.

_____

_____

_____

_____

_____

c. Cultural Relevance

1.Poor people repaired their ripped clothing by
_____ it.

 If a garment was still wearable after being ripped, a poor person would use a piece of old, useless, unwearable fabric to repair the rip in the somewhat decent clothes.

2. Wine makers used _____ skins, such as goat, to store new wine.

3. These are the _____ of Jesus's parables. They are among the few that are in all three synoptic Gospels (Matthew, Mark, and Luke). Jesus told His parables the same time as the Sermon on the Mount and calling His first disciples.

Metaphors were drawn from contemporary culture. Wineskins would stretch with new wine as it continued to ferment and then harden. If new wine was put into a hardened wineskin, fermentation could burst the skin. Similarly, new cloth would be expected to shrink considerably, so using it to patch already-shrunken cloth would be asking for problems. The point, of course, is that He (Jesus) has a new message, the "good news," and if you try to fit it into the old Jewish religion, law, system of animal sacrifices, and so on, it isn't going to fit.

What lesson did Jesus teach with a story about an old coat and an old wineskin?

_____

_____

_____

_____

II. Occasion/Reason why Jesus Told this Parable

The Pharisees asked Jesus two questions:

1. Why do you _____ and _____ with tax collectors and sinners? (Luke 5:30)

2. Why do we (the Pharisees) _____ and you (and your disciples) don't? (Luke 5:33)

In those two questions, we see how "religious" people think. They judge from the outside with self-righteousness and pride. Yet inside they are spiritually poor. The Pharisees wanted to convert the feast into a fast. Jesus addressed the issue through this parable.

III. Main Lessons (Thoughts) to Learn from the Parable

    a.   Jesus came to _____ something new, NOT to build on the old.

    b.   Jesus didn't come to _____ something old, but He came to give us something new.

    c.   Jesus warns against _____ the old and new together.

    d.   Jesus didn't come to continue the Old Testament (The Law), but to _____ it.

    e.   God _____ seeks something new, and He seeks to renew.

NOTES:_____

_____

_____

IV. Composition of the Parable

1. **Garment** = We see _____ applications for what garments can mean throughout scripture.

    a.   _____ (old and new salvation)

"*I will greatly rejoice in the LORD, My soul shall be joyful in my God; For He has clothed me with the garments of salvation, He has covered me with the robe of righteousness.*" (Isaiah 61:10)

b. _____ (old and new Adam, anointed priest)

"For as many of you as were baptized into Christ have put on Christ." (Galatians 3:27)

c. _____ (old and new way to cover from shame)

We see this demonstrated in Genesis with Adam and Eve and then again in the book of Mark with the man who was demon possessed.

"⁷ Then the eyes of both of them were opened, and they knew that they were naked; and they sewed fig leaves together and made themselves coverings." "²¹ Also for Adam and his wife the Lord God made tunics of skin, and clothed them." (Genesis 3:7, 21)

"Then they came to Jesus, and saw the one who had been demon-possessed and had the legion, sitting and clothed and in his right mind. And they were afraid." (Mark 5:15)

2. **Wine**

   i. _____ **Covenant**   *The Blood*

   ii. **The** _____ **of Jesus**   *of the Covenant*

"For this is my blood, which confirms the covenant between God and his people. It is poured out as a sacrifice to forgive

the sins of many." (Matthew 26:28 NLT)

iii. _____ **Spirit –**

> "*And don't be drunk with wine, in which is dissipation; but be filled with the Spirit.*" (Ephesians 5:18 NKJV)

NOTES:_____

_____

_____

V.   Discussion:

1. Understanding the Full Story

During his earthly ministry, Jesus often reached out to help people who were excluded or marginalized by Jewish society of the time. This aspect of Jesus's activities is given special emphasis in the Gospel of Luke. It is Luke who records the well-known words of Jesus, "For the Son of Man came to seek and to save what was lost" (Luke 19:10 NIV).

Our Savior's concern for the outcast is evident in His selection of the tax collector Levi (Matthew) as one of the Twelve, a select group of disciples (Luke 6:12-16). Tax collectors were agents of the Roman government and often became wealthy at the expense of their countrymen by charging excessive amounts. As a result, they were typically despised by their fellow Jews.

When we read this parable in the book of Luke, the tax collector's name was Levi. But, in the book of Matthew, the tax collector's name was Matthew. "Hmm, you might be thinking, 'Is this a mistake?'" No, Levi was his birth name, but because he was a tax collector working for the _____, he was given the name Matthew, possibly by the Romans.

When Jesus asked Matthew to become his disciple, the tax collector did not hesitate. Giving up his lucrative position, he "left everything" (Luke 5:28) and did not look back. He was so honored and gratified by Jesus's invitation that he celebrated with a farewell banquet at his home with Matthew's "unsavory" friends (Luke 5:29). This banquet provided the setting for another of the Master's memorable parables.

The Pharisees saw Jesus eating dinner and questioned how Jesus, as a religious man, could socialize with tax collectors and sinners. The religious leaders also grumbled about why they fast, and John the Baptist's disciples fasted, but Jesus's disciples didn't fast.

2. Why the Pharisees hated tax collectors

Tax collectors worked for Caesar, taking money from Jews to give to the Romans; therefore, they were considered traitors. In addition, they collected more than what was _____ in order to increase their earnings unjustly.

Pharisees considered tax collectors:

1. _____ because of their dishonest ways.

"And when the Pharisees saw it, they said to His disciples, "Why does your Teacher eat with tax collectors and sinners?" (Matthew 9:11)

2. _____ because many of them didn't believe in God of the Bible.

"And if he refuses to hear them, tell it to the church. But if he refuses even to hear the church, let him be to you like a heathen and a tax collector." (Matthew 18:17)

3. _____ or prostitutes because society considered them in the same class.

"Jesus said to them, 'Assuredly, I say to you that tax collectors and harlots enter the kingdom of God before you.'" (Matthew 21:31)

Something old and something new:

Clearly the parable talks about something old and something new.

1. Jesus came to make _____ new. Jesus didn't come to fix the Old Testament (covenant); He

came with a new covenant.

2. The Old Testament was _____ from God. And the problem wasn't in the law, but it was and still is in man and the matters of the heart! Man even broke the law before he received it.

Illustration: If you went to the best chef in the world, gave him a rotten piece of meat and asked him to make you a good steak, he could not. Most likely, he would ask you to give him a "new" steak. You just cannot fix meat once it rots. Similarly, man became rotten due to sin. There is no way we can be good again unless we are renewed or re-created.

3. The Old Testament was a covenant between _____ and _____. That's why Job 14:4 says: "Who can bring a clean *thing* out of an unclean? No one!" God is faithful and will do what He says He will do. But man always breaks the covenant. God is not going to take part of a new testament or covenant and fix the old one; instead, He will create a new testament/covenant.

4. The New Testament is more of a covenant between God the _____ and _____. We accept Jesus's death as payment for our sins and get to partake of the benefits if we receive Him.

5. In the Old Testament, God instructs man to offer sacrifices to be _____. In the New Testament God did everything for us to be saved. And on the cross Jesus said, it was done, complete, finished. No further sacrifices can compare to the price paid for humanity's redemption by the Messiah.

6. The New Testament is completely different. Jesus didn't come to _____ the Old Testament; He came to make everything new.

7. The Old Testament was prophesying to the people that something _____ that would happen, so Jesus came to fulfill the law and not to continue the Old Testament with another era. Jesus was not another prophet.

Old Creation and New Creation

We can divide this parable into three sections.

I. New garment and old garment

II. New wineskin and old wineskin

III. Old and new wine

Similar to the three parables in Luke 15, we see distinctive delineation in this parable inferring something different.

The garment is from the _____, while wine is on the _____. Jesus is saying that being a Christian changes something on the outside and the inside.

Garment:

- To _____ shame

Adam felt naked after sinning. They made fig leaf covers, God instead made a garment to cover his shame. Sin brings shame, a new garment covers shame. Adam tried to cover himself, but God made a suitable covering for them.

Wine:

- The _____ of the Holy Spirit

"And do not be drunk with wine, in which is dissipation; but be filled with the Spirit." (Ephesians 5:18)

When disciples were baptized by the Holy Spirit, people thought they were drunk. (Acts 2 & 3)

No Mixing

1. The Holy Spirit will not _____ an old heart.

2. Some people think they don't need to be saved. They can just do work, and that will make the Holy Spirit reside in them. Works will not re-create you "_____". Only the blood of Jesus can make you wholly "new" again.

3. Our old bodies cannot see God and _____, but when we are re-created, we can communicate with the Holy Spirit.

    i.   Imagine you take a new garment and cut a piece to _____ an old garment. You will ruin both garments as the new one stretches and causes the old one to rip more.

    ii.   An old wineskin has been _____; new wine will stretch it more and break it. You will ruin the old wineskin and spill the new wine.

    iii.   You cannot mix Judaism with Christianity. Christianity is not a _____ of

Judaism, it is new. Yet, the Old Testament still is the word of God. The New Testament is the fulfillment of the Old.

Judging without trying

"And no one, having drunk old wine, immediately desires new; for he says, 'The old is better.'" (Luke 5:39)

a. Those who judge the new wine _____ trying it.

b. These religious people like to _____ good without trying Jesus. They would rather stick with what looks good than what tastes good.

The Author of salvation who covered our shame:

a. Old Garment = what was _____ Christ

b. New Garment = comes _____ the birth of Christ

Jesus answered with this parable to be clear that He didn't come to fix sinners who have gone away from God. Instead, He came to renew (create a new creation). That's the main difference between Jesus and ALL other prophets.

"Create in me a clean heart, O God, and renew a steadfast spirit within me." (Psalm 51:10)

Old	New
Earthly call Earthly blessings	Heavenly call Spiritual blessings
Legalistic walk with curses as consequences	Spiritual walk with God who helps us
Worship by sacrifices	Worship in spirit and truth
Adam and Eve were expelled from the Garden,	The thief on the cross entered paradise
Earthly promises (your children will inherit – and I will give you and your children. etc.)	Heavenly promises – new land, new Heaven, new bodies
Priests must be from the tribe of Levi	Jesus welcomes anyone who accepts Him as Lord as a priest and king
Man was a servant to God	Man partners with God and is the recipient of the inheritance
Will remember your sins to the fourth generation (Deuteronomy 5:9)	Will no longer remember your sins (Hebrews 8:12)
To be born of a Jewish family	To be born of above (reborn)
Mt Sinai, 50th day after the law came down, 3,000 people died (Exodus 32:28)	Mt Zion, 50th day after the resurrection (The Day of Pentecost) the Holy Spirit came down, 3,000 people were saved (Acts 2:41)

VI.   Conclusion:

None of us likes to give up something familiar or comfortable. This is even more true when this "something" has been controlling our view of reality, morality, and religion. So we have a tendency to plug in a new good experience or teaching into our old religious context and make it fit. Jesus's point here is that what He brings cannot be made to fit in the old order and old forms of religion familiar to the Jews. To do that would be destructive to both the old and new. What Jesus brings is new, fresh, and transformational. It will rip apart anything that tries to force it into another way of doing, perceiving, and experiencing. Becoming a Christ follower—a Christian—is a whole new life, not just another religion to be thrown into the world mix of faiths. This is as true today as it was more than 2,000 years ago.

Christianity is not a continuation of Judaism. Instead, the Old Testament is the final chapter of God's plan that started with Adam. Jesus didn't come to fix the Old Testament or to patch it. If Jesus did that, then this would be another religious system. Christianity is a new life through Jesus Christ.

VII. Homework / Memory Verse

Make it Personal: Since I was born into sin and dead in my sins, I needed a new life. I cannot patch my life with prayers, gifts, fasting, or attending church as my old self. I need a new life and a new heart. Prayers, gifts, fasting, or attending church are not the path to salvation; they are the proof of salvation.

In what ways does following Christ require us to replace old habits with new ones? Why do we resist making these changes?

_____

_____

_____

_____

_____

_____

_____

_____

_____

_____

_____

_____

VIII. Middle-Eastern Recipe

LIMONATTA

Egyptian Lime and Mint Drink

This is not your typical lemonade. You will certainly taste the citrus in this traditionally, less sweet and more tangy beverage. The tart flavor is rounded out with delicious orange blossom water (if available) and fresh mint.

INGREDIENTS:

- ½ cup fresh squeezed lime juice (approximately 4 to 8 limes, I prefer key limes)
- 4 cups water
- ½ cup of sugar or ¼ cup agave nectar, add more to taste
- ¼ cup finely diced mint leaves (reserve some sprogs for garnish)
- 2 teaspoons orange blossom water
- 2 cups crushed ice

METHOD:

1. Wash and zest the limes then cut in half. Reserve a few thin slices of lime for garnish. Juice with a press or by hand. Remember, if it's too tart for your taste, you can always add more water or sugar later.
2. Combine the water, lime juice, zest, sugar, orange blossom water and mint in a blender on medium speed for 1-2 minutes. Allow the sweetener to dissolve and the mint to integrate thoroughly.
3. Pour mint limeade into a glass pitcher over crushed ice. Garnish with mint leaves and lime slices. Serve and enjoy!

CHAPTER 6

Parables Talents
DECODED
Of Jesus

I. Bible Passage

a. Reading: Matthew 25:14-30 (ESV)

[14] "For it will be like a man going on a journey, who called his servants and entrusted to them his property. [15] To one he gave five talents, to another two, to another one, to each according to his ability. Then he went away. [16] He who had received the five talents went at once and traded with them, and he made five talents more. [17] So also he who had the two talents made two talents more. [18] But he who had received the one talent went and dug in the ground and hid his master's money. [19] Now after a long time the master of those servants came and settled accounts with them. [20] And he who had received the five talents came forward,

bringing five talents more, saying, 'Master, you delivered to me five talents; here, I have made five talents more.' [21] His master said to him, 'Well done, good and faithful servant. You have been faithful over a little; I will set you over much. Enter into the joy of your master.' [22] And he also who had the two talents came forward, saying, 'Master, you delivered to me two talents; here, I have made two talents more.' [23] His master said to him, 'Well done, good and faithful servant. You have been faithful over a little; I will set you over much. Enter into the joy of your master.' [24] He also who had received the one talent came forward, saying, 'Master, I knew you to be a hard man, reaping where you did not sow, and gathering where you scattered no seed, [25] so I was afraid, and I went and hid your talent in the ground. Here, you have what is yours.' [26] But his master answered him, 'You wicked and slothful servant! You knew that I reap where I have not sown and gather where I scattered no seed? [27] Then you ought to have invested my money with the bankers, and at my coming I should have received what was my own with interest. [28] So take the talent from him and give it to him who has the ten talents. [29] For to everyone who has will more be given, and he will have an abundance. But from the one who has not, even what he has will be taken away. [30] And cast the worthless servant into the outer darkness. In that place there will be weeping and gnashing of teeth.'"

b. Explanation of the Parable

A rich man who was going away on a journey called three of his servants and gave them some treasure he entrusted them to invest. One servant received five talents, the second servant received two talents, and the third received one talent, based on each one's ability. After a long time, the master returned and asked each servant of their achievement with the investment. The master was pleased with the two servants who invested and invited them to go into the joy of their master. The servant who received one talent, complained about how harsh the master was and was penalized for his thinking and lack of action.

c. Cultural Relevance

It was a customary eastern tradition for a master to give his money to his servants to invest for him during his travels. Typically, the talents were apportioned on the basis of the abilities of the servants.

In Jesus's times, the word "talent" referred to money and not an aptitude, ability, skill, or spiritual gift, although that may well be the parallel for us today.

The word "talent" is derived from the Greek word *talanton*, which means balance, sum, weight. So, in fact, the basic root of the word talent as used today to denote the capacity of achievement, success, or ability was originally a unit of weight or money for the payment of goods and services in the ancient world.

II. Occasion/Reason why Jesus Tells this Parable

Jesus uses this opportunity to answer the disciples' question in Matthew 24:3, *"As Jesus was sitting on the Mount of Olives, the disciples came to him privately. 'Tell us,' they said, 'when will this happen, and what will be the sign of your coming and of the end of the age?'"*

III. Main Lessons(Thoughts) to Learn from the Parable

a. To be "_____" and "_____" (from the inside) for the second coming of Jesus Christ

b. Doing the work of the Kingdom is the _____ of every believer

c. Using the talents that God has given us for His

_____

The master says three things to reward each of the first two servants:

1. They received their master's commendation, "Well done, good and faithful servant."

2. Because they had proven themselves to be faithful with the few things entrusted to them, the master gave them even greater responsibilities.

3. They were invited to "enter into the joy of your master," which would seem to be the salvation of lost sinners.

IV. Composition of the Parable

1. **Rich man** = _____Christ

"For you know the grace of our Lord Jesus Christ, that though He was rich, yet for your sakes He became poor, that you through His poverty might become rich." (2 Corinthians 8:9)

2. **Traveling** = Ascending to Heaven, leaving the choice for _____to work or not work for God's kingdom, and to know the truth or not

3. **Servants** = all mankind, _____ believers or non-believers

4. **The servants investing** = believers who are _____ for the King. There are no useless or unimportant organs in our body, likewise, every believer has a specific and a _____ job in the Body of Christ. (see 1 Corinthians 12)

5. **Giving account** = standing before the _____ of Jesus Christ, giving an explanation for how we used our gifts and talents

"For we must all appear before the judgment seat of Christ, that

each one may receive the things done in the body, according to what he has done, whether good or bad." (2 Corinthians 5:10)

6. **Talents** = what we have been _____ with or our surroundings. Every person is in charge of what's been given to him/her. In addition, God intentionally puts people in our path for us to influence. Do we take the opportunities?

7. **Silver** = the _____ of God

"The words of the Lord are pure words, like silver tried in a furnace of earth, purified seven times." (Psalm 12:6)

Understanding Talents

Biblical scholars do not agree on the value of a talent. It is a unit of weight and can be applied to precious metals. In the Bible, talents are made of silver or gold. Silver was typically used for purchasing and investing. Even its modern weight is debated. A Greek talent weighs 57 pounds, Roman 71 pounds, Babylonian 67 pounds, and Egyptian 60 pounds. Some sources say a common New Testament talent weighed 75.6 pounds, while others say 130 pounds. We will use the Roman equivalent because during Jesus's time they were under Roman rule. We will use the silver talent to understand the value of talents. As of March 2018, a pound of silver is valued at $198.28 and a pound of gold has a value of $21,120.00

1 Talent = 71 Pounds of Silver = $14,077.88

---

8. **Gold** = _____and the glory of God

Talents and Gifts:

Everyone has at least one talent, and God will equip you with the right gifts to work and invest with your talents.

Abilities + Opportunities = _____

V. Discussion

1. God looks for _____not just

_____.

Take a moment to read the story of the widow's two mites.

"Now Jesus sat opposite the treasury and saw how the people put money into the treasury. And many who were rich put in much. [42] Then one poor widow came and threw in two mites, which make a quadrans. [43] So He called His disciples to Himself and said to them, "Assuredly, I say to you that this poor widow has put in more than all those who have given to the treasury; [44] for they all put in out of their abundance, but she out of her poverty put in all that she had, her whole livelihood." (Mark 12:41-44)

Compare what the master said to the servants who received five and two talents. Name any differences! (verses 21 and verses 23)

_____

_____

_____

    2. We can NO LONGER _____for ourselves. We must use the talents God has given us.

"And He died for all, that those who live should live no longer for themselves, but for Him who died for them and rose again." (2 Corinthians 5:15)

    3. Using your talents with excellence has a _____.

    4. Four important elements comprise this parable: _____, _____, _____, and _____.

        a. **Time** is significant in Jesus's teaching about His return at the end of the age, beginning in Matthew 24. Jesus made clear that His return would not be immediate, but would be only after much trouble and the passing of a considerable period of time. While there would be signs to discern the general "season" of His return, neither the day nor the hour would be known (see Matthew 24:30-31). Beyond this, His return would come at a time when it was not expected.

b. **Money**. This parable tells us that both believers and unbelievers are entrusted with certain things, and that they must give account for their stewardship. Everyone is accountable to God for how they use (or do not use) resources that God has entrusted to them.

c. **Work**. Both the first and second servants immediately set to work with the master's money. The money does not go to work, as such, but the worker. When the third servant's excuses are set aside, the master sees that he is lazy – he didn't do any work.

d. **Profit**. Those who work with what they are entrusted, in order to make a profit for their master, are rewarded for their faithfulness.

The unfaithful lose not only their reward but their stewardship. Interestingly, we find this same principle stated in connection with the parable of the soils found in Matthew 13:12, Mark 4:25, and Luke 8:18. The soil that produces no grain (in other instances, no fruit or profit) is bad soil. Only the soil that produces a crop is "good" soil. (The parable of the soils is found in Parables Decoded Volume 1: Appearances)

5. Being wicked, evil, and _____will cause the servant to bury God's Living Word (silver). The result is that the unfaithful servant never understands who God is or uses what He has entrusted to him. The servant didn't know who the Lord was - **so he said:**

   a. **"Lord, I knew you"...** did he know the Lord or did he know _____the Lord, since he buried the silver (God's Word)?

"Jesus answered and said to them, "You are mistaken, not knowing the Scriptures nor the power of God." (Matthew 22:29)

b. **"To be a hard <u>man</u>"** - he didn't know that   he   was   talking   to

_____.

c. **"Hard"**- if he sat with the Word of God, he would have found that God is _____and full of love. God is gentle and kind, full of goodness and mercy.

d. **"Reaping where you have not sown, and gathering where you have not scattered seed"** -   God   is   generous   in

_____.

e. **"And I was afraid"** - Fear is the _____of burying God's Word. Fear is also the result of lack of love.

"There is no fear in love. But perfect love drives out fear, because fear has to do with punishment. The one who fears is not made perfect in love." (1 John 4:18)

    f. We need to be awake at all times, serving God with _____ and quality.

The third slave is lazy and useless, as opposed to hard- working, and useful. He does not "go to work" with his master's money, and make a profit. He does no work for a long time and proves himself useless.

Question: What happened to the one talent that the servant gave back to the master?

_____

_____

Ways to bury your talents

1. Feeling _____ with the talents God gave you
2. _____ what God has given someone else
3. Knowing the talents God gave you and doing _____ with them

4. Wasting the _____and relationships God puts in your path

5. Holding onto _____

Can you think of other ways?

_____

_____

Ways to use your talents

1. _____and understanding God's Word

2. Attending and participating in _____

3. Stepping up when _____ step away

4. Doing _____ the ministry needs to keep moving forward

5. Using what God gave you to _____ His kingdom

6. Spreading the _____

7. Living a "true" Christian _____ so your friends and neighbors see Jesus in you

8. _____to God. Your life can be the best "sermon" others can see or hear

Can you think of other ways?

_____

_____

God rejoices in His servants making a profit. What does a profit mean to God?

_____

_____

If we were to make an equation of this parable, it would probably look like this:

Resources (talents) + Labor (work) + Time = Profit

Just as a businessman expects to make a profit and is happy when his employees increase his wealth, so God expects a profit and rejoices in it. He has granted the time and resources for men to make a profit for the Kingdom of Heaven until He returns. The question for us to consider is this: Just how do we measure "spiritual profit"?

I think we could all agree that:

1. The salvation of lost souls is a profit for the kingdom. Thus, evangelism is one form of spiritual profit.

Ephesians 4:11-13 says, *"It was he who gave some to be apostles, some to be prophets, some to be evangelists, and some to be pastors and teachers, to prepare God's people for works of service, so that the body of Christ may be built up until we all reach unity in the faith and in the knowledge of the Son of God and become mature, attaining to the whole measure of the fullness of Christ."*

2. Edification or spiritual growth is also profitable for the Kingdom of Heaven.
3. Bringing glory to God is profitable.

"So whether you eat or drink, or whatever you do, do everything for the glory of God." (1 Corinthians 10:31).

Question - What are your five best traits or greatest qualities?

_____

_____

_____

_____

_____

VI.   Conclusion

The talents that the Lord has entrusted you with are perfect for you. If you feel you can handle or deserve more, be faithful with the little you have, and the Lord will make you in charge of much. Jesus is coming back, so be ready and invest with the talents you have and/or those around you.

This parable insists that watchfulness must not lead to passivity but to doing one's God-given duties. Everyone has received gifts according to their abilities and what they make of these gifts is what counts in the end. We must continually learn, grow, and carry out our responsibilities and develop the resources that God entrusts to us until He returns and settles accounts. As in the earlier parables, we see a progression in the theme of being prepared for Christ's return, with each parable having a different nuance in its lesson.

Not how much talent one has but how one uses that talent is important to God. It is not how many gifts God gives to a person but what one does with them.

Can you summarize this parable as to what it means to you today in a sentence or two?

_____

_____

_____

VII. Homework / Memory Verse

1. Discover your talent(s). The Word of God assures us that we are all given talents. Don't despise what you have.

    _____

    _____

    _____

    _____

2. Where are you able to invest your talents (money and abilities)? What groups or individuals can benefit most from the talents you have?

_____

_____

_____

_____

_____

3. The purpose of life is not to eat, drink, and be merry! The purpose of life is to be fruitful and can be summarized in the following two passages:

- Matthew 22:36-40 – *"Teacher, which is the greatest commandment in the Law?" Jesus replied: "'Love the Lord your God with all your heart and with all your soul and with all your mind.' The second is like it: 'Love your neighbor as yourself.' All the Law and the Prophets hang on these two commandments."*

- 1 Corinthians 10:31 – *"So whether you eat or drink or whatever you do, do it all for the glory of God."*

With the purpose of life in mind, how can you apply these scriptures to your life today in a new way?

_____

_____

_____

_____

_____

4. Is it important to God how much talent you have? (see 2 Corinthians 8:10-12)

_____

_____

_____

_____

_____

_____

VII.   Middle-Eastern Recipe

Kufta Kabob *(Ground Meat Kabob)*

Kufta Kabob is a staple in the Middle East and a must-try recipe. Ground beef and lamb mixed with fresh parsley, onions, garlic and Middle Eastern spices comes together in less than thirty minutes. If ground lamb isn't accessible or preferred you may substitute ground beef.

INGREDIENTS

1 medium yellow onion, quartered
2 garlic cloves
1 whole bunch parsley, stems removed (about 2 cups parsley leaves)
1 pound ground beef
½ pound ground lamb
¼ cup breadcrumbs moistened with water
Salt and pepper
1 ½ teaspoon ground allspice

½ teaspoon cayenne pepper
½ teaspoon ground sumac (optional)
½ teaspoon paprika
Pita bread to serve

METHOD

1. Soak 10 wooden skewers in water for about 1 hour; remove from the water when you are ready to begin. Lightly oil the grates of a gas grill and preheat it to medium high for about 20 minutes.
2. In a food processor, chop the onion, garlic, and parsley.
3. Add the beef, lamb, breadcrumbs, and the spices. Run the processor until all is well-combined, forming a pasty meat mixture.
4. Remove the meat mixture from the food processor and place in a large bowl. Take a handful portion of the meat mixture and mold it on a wooden skewer. Repeat the process until you use all of the meat. For best results, make sure each kufta kebab is about 1 inch thick.
5. Lay the skewered kufta kebabs on a tray lined with parchment paper.
6. Place the kufta kebabs on the lightly oiled, heated gas grill. Grill on medium-high heat for 4 minutes on one side, turn over and grill for another 3-4 minutes.
7. Serve the kufta kebabs immediately with pita bread, tahini sauce, diced tomatoes, and cucumbers to your liking.

CONCLUSION

Parables
dECODED
of Jesus

As we reflect upon our journey together through these five parables, let us take a bird's-eye view of the common thread we can find. While we can draw many similarities, we want to elaborate upon the fact that all of these parables appear to provide a simple story. But upon further examination, we see a deeper common truth. We are presented in this grouping of parables a common theme of old and new.

In these parables we see old and new covenants being confronted, old and new thinking defied, and even the old and new way of doing things opposed. Jesus is calling us not to an old standard but a higher one based on grace not built on our own worth, goodness, or righteous actions.

In these parables we see that it doesn't matter how much talent you are endowed with but rather what you do with it. Nor does it matter when you are called to work in the field. The reward is God's to give, and it is centered upon our wholehearted response to the invitation.

God is perhaps asking us not to do what is traditional, but instead what is pleasing and aligns with His heart. God is challenging us through the stories Jesus told to encounter our preconceived notions about eternity and be open to His "new" way that was defined from the beginning of time.

For further study:

After studying the parables, we must

- Live as many lessons behind the parables as we can while we are here on earth.
- Use what we learned for God to give us personal devotions from Bible readings.
- Take a parable and choose one word, such as oil, and expand the study of that word from the Scriptures. Meditate on what we learn and see where God leads us. Keep a journal of our studies and the changes we notice to strengthen our faith.
- Examine ourselves daily with the measure of the Word of God. Many of us are guilty, and notice when we examine ourselves in comparison to others. But Jesus wants us to

start examining ourselves against His Word. If I compare myself to a drug lord or a mass murderer, I might get the impression that I'm perfect. But the Bible is the true measure of my thoughts, acts, and deeds. Therefore, daily, we need to look at ourselves in the mirror and ask if we are pretending to be who we are? If my life were on a big screen 24/7 in front of other people who could see every thought and action, would I do the same things I'm doing now? Many of us examine ourselves against bad patterns, and we judge ourselves much better than "them". But Jesus wants us to examine our good habits, because they might look good but are actually corrupt.

Notes:

_____

_____

_____

_____

_____

_____

_____

_____

_____

_____

_____

_____

_____

_____

_____

Notes:

ANSWERS

ANSWER KEY:

Introduction to the Parables:

Key Elements of the Parables

1. preached
2. 43-58
3. one-third
4. preserved
5. practical
6. response
7. Parables can be categorized in three sections:
   a. God, you
   b. believers
   c. non

4 Questions that Frequently Arise about the Parables:
1. mean
2. parables
3. speak
4. interpret

Q1. What does "parable" mean?

1. place   cast
2. like   looks
3. proverb

Definition of Parable:
illustrative
comparison

Q2. What are the parables?

Parables are:

      1.   nature life
      2.   simple brief
      3.   history   culture
      4.   Earthly   Heavenly
      5.   secrets
      6.   education
      7.   clarify
      8.   multitudes

Q3. Why did Christ speak in parables?

      1.   hunger
      2.   dull   hear
      3.   special
      4.   separate

Q4. How do we interpret the parables?

      1.   Analyze
      2.   interpretation
      3.   assume
      4.   cultural   historical
      5.   overanalyze
      6.   arrange
      7.   glean
      8.   understand
      9.   solely

Chapter 2: The Good Samaritan

c. Cultural Relevance:

> <u>Torah</u>
> <u>unclean</u>

Geography:

> <u>neighbors</u>

II. Occasion/Reason why Jesus tells this Parable:

<u>inherit</u>

III. Main lessons (thoughts) from the parable

a.	<u>birth</u>	e.	<u>neighbor</u>
b.	<u>perfectly</u>	f.	<u>justify</u>
c.	<u>need</u>	g.	<u>biblical</u>
d.	<u>regardless</u>		

IV. Composition of the parable

a.	<u>place</u>	f.	<u>religion</u>
b.	<u>Satan</u>	g.	<u>price</u>
c.	<u>winning</u>	h.	<u>place</u>
d.	<u>sin</u>	i.	<u>anointing</u>
e.	<u>live</u>	j.	<u>Holy</u>

V. Discussion:
<u>heart</u>

Participants: <u>action</u>

1.	<u>Lawyer</u>	4.	<u>Priest</u>
2.	<u>Traveler</u>	5.	<u>Levites</u>

3. Thieves

Excuses:

      d. wounded   e. time

      e. mentality   f. accused

      f. trick   g. else

      g. time

Extraordinary measures taken by the Samaritan:

1. responsible   5. planning

2. helping   6. provision

3. benefit   7. gratitude

4. money

CHAPTER 3: The Fig Tree

c. Cultural Relevance
    1. vineyard
    2. hotheaded
    3. crowded
    4. prosperity
    5. sickness wa

II. Occasion/Reason why Jesus tells this Parable

    a. after

b.   question

c.   turns

III. Main lessons/Thoughts to Learn from the parable

    a.   fruit

    b.   reason

    c.   delay

    d.   judge

    e.   both

    f.   repent

IV. Composition of the parable

a. God	e. time
b. Jesus	f. word
c. world	g. fruit
d. Fig	

A. Some Facts about Fig Trees

i.   third When

ii.   most

iii.   two

iv.   first

v.   second

vi.   blossom

vii. before

viii. prosperity

ix. symbolizes

A. Invitation to Repent

i.   sin

    ii. could
   iii. both
   iv. pleased
    v. allows
   vi. repent

B. Invitation to be Fruitful

    i. hypocrisy
   ii. individual
  iii. fruitless
   iv. nature

C. Invitation to use the Advocate (Jesus)

    i. advocate
   ii. Jesus
  iii. interceding

CHAPTER 4: Parable of the Workers in the Vineyard

c. Cultural Relevance

a. automatically   c. rich
b. outside   d. justify

III. Main Lessons/Thoughts to Learn from the Parable

  a. Salvation
  b. Ministry
  c. complain
  d. faithfully
  e. unjust

IV. Composition of the Parable
1. God
2. wait
3. Hours
4. Denarius
5. World
6. Jesus
7. field
8. salvation
9. belongs

V. Discussion (Please Note...)
1. avoiding
2. wait

Salvation is for everyone:
1. invite
2. right
3. interpretation

Accept Ministry (serving):
1. forever
2. first   last

The Lord wants you to serve Him with:.

1. time
2. money
3. health
4. Everything

Don't wait to be:

1. invited
2. in worthy
3. talented
4. Spiritual
5. old

Chapter 5: The Patch and The Wineskins p

b. Explanation of the Parable

three   think differently

c. Cultural Relevance

1. patching
2. animal
3. first

II. Occasion/Reason why Jesus Told This Parable

1. eat   drink
2. fast

III. Main Lesson (Thoughts) to Learn from the Parable

a. establish   d. fulfill
b.   fix   e. always
c. mixing

IV. Composition of the Parable

1. three
   a. Salvation   b. Christ   c. Cover

2. i. New   ii. Blood   iii. Holy

V. Discussion

1. Understanding the Full Story
   Romans
2. Why the Pharisees hated Tax Collectors
   owed

Pharisees Considered Tax Collectors:

1. Sinners   2. Heathens   3. Harlots

Something Old & Something New:

1. Everything
2. Holy
3. God   Man
4. Father   Jesus
5. Saved
6. Patch
7. New

Old and New Creation:

outside   inside

Garment – cover

Wine – joy

No Mixing:

1. fill   2. Anew   3. Live

i. fix   ii. Stretched iii. Continuation

Judging Without Trying:

a. without
b. look

The Author of Salvation who Covered our Shame:

a. before
b. after

Chapter 6: The Talents

III. Main lesson of this Parable

a. <u>Waiting</u>   <u>ready</u>

b. <u>responsibility</u>

c. <u>glory</u>

IV. Composition of the Parable

1. <u>Jesus</u>

2. <u>mankind</u>

3. <u>committed</u>

4. <u>working</u>   <u>unique</u>

5. <u>throne/seat</u>

6. <u>equipped</u>

7. <u>word</u>

8. <u>Heaven</u>

Abilities + Opportunity = <u>**Responsibility**</u>

IV.   Discussion

1. <u>Quality</u>   <u>Quantity</u>

2. <u>live</u>

3. <u>reward</u>

4. <u>Time</u>, <u>Money</u>, <u>Work</u>,   <u>Profit</u>

5. <u>lazy</u>

    a. <u>about</u>

    b. <u>God</u>

    c. <u>love</u>

    d. <u>giving</u>

    e. <u>result</u>

f. <u>faithfulness</u>

Ways to Bury your Talents:

1. <u>Discontented</u>

2. <u>Envying</u>

3. <u>Nothing</u>

4. <u>People</u>

5. <u>Hurts</u>

Ways to Use Your Talents:

1. <u>reading</u>
2. <u>church</u>
3. <u>others</u>
4. <u>whatever</u>
5. <u>advance</u>
6. <u>gospel</u>
7. <u>life</u>
8. <u>yielding</u>

ABOUT THE AUTHORS:

HANY & DIANA ASAAD have a Middle Eastern upbringing and understand the culture distinctly with degrees in Biblical Studies. They have been in Christian ministry (including Arabic) for more than twenty years and are excited to bring this knowledge to a new audience in a relevant and original way. They have been guests on international television programs and satellite TV channels associated with *The 700 Club, Joyce Meyer Ministries* and *TBN*. They currently reside in the South with their three beautiful daughters.

Learn More at:
www.RelentlessLiving.com
www.HanyAsaad.com
www.DianaAsaad.com

Also Available: